IF FOU

MW01632195

# GREATER THAN A TOURIST BOOK SERIES REVIEWS FROM READERS

I think the series is wonderful and beneficial for tourists to get information before visiting the city.

-Seckin Zumbul, Izmir Turkey

I am a world traveler who has read many trip guides but this one really made a difference for me. I would call it a heartfelt creation of a local guide expert instead of just a guide.

-Susy, Isla Holbox, Mexico

New to the area like me, this is a must have!

-Joe, Bloomington, USA

This is a good series that gets down to it when looking for things to do at your destination without having to read a novel for just a few ideas.

-Rachel, Monterey, USA

Good information to have to plan my trip to this destination.

-Pennie Farrell, Mexico

Great ideas for a port day.

-Mary Martin USA

Aptly titled, you won't just be a tourist after reading this book. You'll be greater than a tourist!

-Alan Warner, Grand Rapids, USA

Even though I only have three days to spend in San Miguel in an upcoming visit, I will use the author's suggestions to guide some of my time there. An easy read - with chapters named to guide me in directions I want to go.

-Robert Catapano, USA

Great insights from a local perspective! Useful information and a very good value!

-Sarah, USA

This series provides an in-depth experience through the eyes of a local. Reading these series will help you to travel the city in with confidence and it'll make your journey a unique one.

-Andrew Teoh, Ipoh, Malaysia

# GREATER THAN A TOURIST –SAN ANTONIO TEXAS USA

*50 Travel Tips from a Local*

Brandi N. Aguillon

Cover designed by: Ivana Stamenkovic
Cover Image: https://pixabay.com/en/san-antonio-city-cityscape-347429/

Greater Than a Tourist
Visit our website at www.GreaterThanaTourist.com

Lock Haven, PA

**ISBN:** 9781983271694

# >TOURIST

50 TRAVEL TIPS FROM A LOCAL

# BOOK DESCRIPTION

Are you excited about planning your next trip?

Do you want to try something new?

Would you like some guidance from a local?

If you answered yes to any of these questions, then this Greater Than a Tourist book is for you.

Greater Than a Tourist- San Antonio Texas USA by Brandi N. Aguillon offers the inside scoop on San Antonio. Most travel books tell you how to travel like a tourist. Although there is nothing wrong with that, as part of the Greater Than a Tourist series, this book will give you travel tips from someone who has lived at your next travel destination.

In these pages, you will discover advice that will help you throughout your stay. This book will not tell you exact addresses or store hours but instead will give you excitement and knowledge from a local that you may not find in other smaller print travel books.

Travel like a local. Slow down, stay in one place, and get to know the people and the culture. By the time you finish this book, you will be eager and prepared to travel to your next destination.

# TABLE OF CONTENTS

12. Cheesy Jane's
13. Paula Deen's
14. Remember the Alamo
15. The River Walk
16. River Tour
17. Medina River Hiking
18. Mission San José
19. Mission Concepción
20. Mission San Juan Capistrano
21. Mission Espada
22. SeaWorld
23. Six Flags Fiesta Texas
24. Kiddie Park
25. Morgan's Wonderland
26. Majestic Theater
27. Downtown Carriage Rides
28. Escape Rooms
29. Tower of Americas
30. San Antonio Rampage
31. Go Spurs Go
32. Golfing
33. Brackenridge Park
34. San Antonio Zoo
35. Japanese Tea Gardens
36. McNay Art Museum
37. The Witte Museum

# DEDICATION

This book is dedicated to my wife and mother. You both drive me nuts and I love you.

Bianca, this book wouldn't have been possible without your constant Texas Pride and continuous encouragement.

Mom, thank you for encouraging me to write for as long as I can remember.

# ABOUT THE AUTHOR

Brandi lives in San Antonio, Texas with her wife (a native to San Antonio), two cats (Chips and Queso) and four sugar gliders (Bruce, Talia, Harley, and Damian). She moved to San Antonio in 2012 for undergrad at Trinity University and currently attends law school. If she had spare time, she would spend it reading, writing, and sleeping.

# HOW TO USE THIS BOOK

The Greater Than a Tourist book series was written by someone who has lived in an area for over three months. The goal of this book is to help travelers either dream or experience different locations by providing opinions from a local. The author has made suggestions based on their own experiences. Please do your own research before traveling to the area in case the suggested places are unavailable.

# FROM THE PUBLISHER

Traveling can be one of the most important parts of a person's life. The anticipation and memories that you have are some of the best. As a publisher of the Greater Than a Tourist book series, as well as the popular 50 Things to Know book series, we strive to help you learn about new places, spark your imagination, and inspire you. Wherever you are and whatever you do I wish you safe, fun, and inspiring travel.

Lisa Rusczyk Ed. D.
CZYK Publishing

# OUR STORY

Traveling is a passion of the "Greater than a Tourist" series creator. Lisa studied abroad in college, and for their honeymoon Lisa and her husband toured Europe. During her travels to Malta, an older man tried to give her some advice based on his own experience living on the island since he was a young boy. She was not sure if she should talk to the stranger but was interested in his advice. When traveling to some places she was wary to talk to locals because she was afraid that they weren't being genuine. Through her travels, Lisa learned how much locals had to share with tourists. Lisa created the "Greater Than a Tourist" book series to help connect people with locals. A topic that locals are very passionate about sharing.

# WELCOME TO
# > TOURIST

# INTRODUCTION

*"San Antonio speaks for itself, and much of its charm is in the way it embodies its past."*

– Novelist, screenwriter, and producer Larry McMurtry. 1968

San Antonio has been described as a big city with a small town feel. It makes for an excellent traveling destination for this reason. While it has its tourist traps, San Antonio has so much more and being in San Antonio means you can live like a local.

History plays a vital role in Texas and the pride that Texans have in their state. San Antonio honors its past while looking to the future.

# 1. FIESTA

Fiesta is an experience unique to San Antonio. Anyone who is not from Texas has trouble understanding the pride that comes from being a native to this big state. In my opinion, Fiesta is an embodiment of that Texas pride. Fiesta is in the middle of April and is 17 days of parties. The history goes back to 1891 but has evolved since then with over 100 events, including music, fantastic food, a four-day block party, and so much more.

The biggest attraction, for some, is the parades. Groups from other cities and states get invited to participate. There are three main parades: The Texas Cavaliers (AKA The River Parade), Battle of Flowers, and the Flambeau Parade (AKA the Night Parade). Battle of Flowers is the only parade in the United States that is produced only by women. Each show has historical significance, but Battle of Flowers is the oldest and goes back to the beginning of Fiesta. The best thing about Fiesta (apart from the menu) is the number of charities and volunteers that get involved in the planning.

Oh, and if you find yourself watching one of the Fiesta Parades, don't forget to yell "Show me your shoes!" at the Fiesta Court (made up of a queen, a princess, and 24 duchesses). These women usually wear long dresses, and it has become a tradition for them to lift their skirts and show their shoes that has turned into a creativity competition with many women showing up with custom boots, slippers, extravagantly decorated flip flops, and other creatively decorated footwear.

## 2. OYSTER BAKE

This is actually part of San Antonio, but it deserves its own section. Oyster Bake is hosted by St. Mary's Texas and is one of my favorite Fiesta events (mainly because it gets me out of a day of school each year). Oyster Bake is two days long and is the kick off to Fiesta. It typically hosts a handful of great bands and terrific food. If you can splurge for the VIP Experience, it's recommended just for the access to air-conditioned restrooms. It also comes with neck and shoulder massages, unlimited snacks and drinks, phone charging stations, and several other goodies.

# 3. KIDCATION

San Antonio becomes a citywide playground for children for a week. This usually takes place in August and is filled with cheap experiences and free activities. There are events at the Art Museum, music and food fairs, free movie screenings with local taco trucks, and much more. The last event held can act as a two for one as there are often school supplies for students as well!

# 4. PRIDE BIGGER THAN TEXAS

If you're in San Antonio at the end of June and are interested in celebrating Pride, then you're welcome to participate in Pride Bigger Than Texas, San Antonio's Pride Parade. The parade is usually held the first Saturday following the fourth Saturday in June. It is considered to be the main Pride event in San Antonio. Organization of the parade is done by Pride San Antonio, Inc., which also produces other events like the San Antonio LGBT International Film Festival and sports tournaments. They also participate and host races and walks to raise money. All money raised by the organization is donated to nonprofit organizations that the Board of Directors chooses.

## 5. GHOST TRACKS

In 1930 there was an accident with a school bus. It was full of children and crossing the train tracks at Villamain and Shane when it stalled. A train then hit the bus. Since then, urban legend says that if you stop your car over the tracks, put it in neutral with your handbrake and engine off, the ghosts of the children will push your vehicle uphill to safety. There's a small decline backward, but legend says that your car will go forward. Native San Antonians say that if sprinkle your back bumper with talcum or baby powder, you'll see the small handprints of the children who push you.

It isn't really a tourist attraction, and it's definitely not the safest activity to do in San Antonio, but it is a popular legend in San Antonio that many natives are passionate about, and many decide to test the theory. I do not recommend you park your car over train tracks. If you're interested in ghost stories, though, it is definitely a place to check out.

# 6. HELICOPTER TOURS

Honestly, the best way to see San Antonio is through the Flights of Fancy Tour, unless you're scared of heights. Alamo Helicopters provides tours of Texas Hill Country, San Antonio City Highlights, and the Alamo Tour (also called the Downtown Tour). It's surprisingly inexpensive for some of the trips and offers a unique perspective of the city. The tour provides a gorgeous view, and one of the best things about it is the chance to get off your feet (and out of the Texas sun!) and really experience the trip.

# 7. BIG LOU'S PIZZA

They say everything is bigger in Texas; this is undoubtedly true of Big Lou's pizza. This is a great place to try if you're visiting with a large group of people. The restaurant itself has a fun atmosphere, but more interesting is there 42-inch pizza—that's the size of a child, one -fourth the length of a Beetle Volkswagen, or an inch shorter than Kenny Baker (AKA R2-D2). More importantly, the massive size of the pizza doesn't detract from its taste.

Big Lou's didn't start out selling giant pizzas, though. The idea came from waiting three hours after ordering a pizza. From there, the idea grew, and Big Lou's was born. It wasn't until the company was doing well that the owner decided to go bigger and ordered an oven that cooked a 37-inch pizza. Sometime later came the 42-inch pizza. If you find yourself hungry in San Antonio, it's definitely worth a stop.

## 8. HONCHOS CHURRO TRUCK

Food trucks are pretty much a staple in Texas. Honestly, some of the best tacos I've ever had have come from a food truck. Entering into the mix is Honchos. It started as a small business; they were only open a few days a week, but they've since grown in popularity and are open most days in the afternoon. Honchos serves one thing, and one thing only: Churros. Delicious, sweet fried dough and they've since expanded to the chocolate churro.

Their churros are warm, toasty, and you can fill them with any sauce from their list. The frozen churro, though, is where your focus should be. The sauce will eventually seep out of your churro, and when it does, rather than dripping into a mess on the paper it tops your vanilla ice cream. The frozen churro is two smaller churros, sticking out of delicious vanilla ice cream. When you're there, don't forget to take a picture with the truck sign that reads, "I got churroed"

# 9. TIP TOP CAFE

Tip Top is another historical sight of San Antonio. It's been serving chicken fried steak since the thirties. The prices are reasonable, the food is delicious, and their onion rings are massive. It is a small, out of the way place that appeared on the show Diners, Drive-Ins, and Dives comfort food episode. The restaurant is a place for the locals and better than most tourist traps that offer food.

# 10. RESTAURANT WEEK

Restaurant Week is probably one of the coolest events. It's done in many different cities, and it's a great way to try the local food--even the expensive places—for a great price. Essentially several restaurants in the San Antonio area participate, and you can purchase tickets from one of two tiers (Tier One being more expensive, and Tier Two being a little cheaper). Then, you pick a restaurant (reservations are recommended, though not required) and there's a three-course menu that you get to choose from, based on your tier. San Antonio has a lot of expensive restaurants, and it's a fun way to try something a little different without breaking the bank.

Even better, by participating in restaurant week, you're giving back to the city! For every meal ordered participating restaurants will donate $1 for lunch and $2 for dinner to Culinaria, the organization that organizes the event, and the programs it supports.

## 11. GUENTHER HOUSE

A museum, gift shop, banquet hall, and restaurant, all rolled into one beautiful restaurant. Guenther House is a pretty big hit among tourists and San Antonians alike, so if you're looking for a quick bite, this wouldn't be the place to go. However, if you're willing to wait a little bit, the experience is absolutely worth it. They are known for their large cinnamon rolls, delicious biscuits and gravy, and an "All

American Breakfast." Their website estimates that they serve over 200,000 guests a year, but still manage spectacular quality of food and service. It is on the more expensive side of dining compared to some breakfast places, but the experience absolutely compensates.

Guenther House has its start in the Flour Mills, and you can explore the history of both the land and the city while you wait to eat. Outdoor seating is available and if the weather is nice enough, highly recommended.

## 12. CHEESY JANE'S

If you don't order a milkshake while you're here, I have failed at my job. The staff there is great; they are incredibly friendly and welcoming. The decor is fun, the food is terrific and cheap, and any place that has the options for tater tots is doing something right. I went to school at Trinity University, not too far from this little diner, and it was a great spot to go when I wanted something that was less cafeteria food. Everything tastes fresh and yummy, and despite being a small little diner, it is probably one of my favorite restaurants in San Antonio. It is also positioned in a great location near Brackenridge Park, the zoo, and a few other San Antonio favorites.

# 13. PAULA DEEN'S

Paula Deen's is a recent addition to San Antonio. I've only been there once, and it was an experience to remember! You'll want to come here with your appetites because the food is incredible and it will just keep coming.

For lunch, your table gets to choose two main dishes and three sides. For dinner, your table chooses three main dishes and four sides. Welcome to Family Style dining. No need to worry if you don't get to try something and it's all gone, flag down your waiter and order some more because the food is endless. I had a hard time choosing what my favorite was, but I will recommend the fried chicken and the mashed potatoes. You'll be full, but don't forget to order dessert! The chocolate ooey-gooey was heaven, but if you don't have much of a sweet tooth, the banana pudding is creamy and smooth. I enjoyed both, and I don't even like banana pudding.

# 14. REMEMBER THE ALAMO

You were probably wondering when this would show up, or if it even would, but honestly, a travel book about San Antonio would be incomplete without mentioning the Alamo. I would be shunned from the city if I forgot to include it. Is it a tourist trap? Absolutely. Should you still go? Definitely. If there is one thing most people know about San Antonio, it's that the Alamo exists. You'll likely be mocked if you skip it on a trip into the city.

If you have any interest in history, the Alamo is actually an engaging place to visit. They have different collections of memorabilia, various events, interactive content and a few different tour options. There are some requests, to show your respect to the history there, so take a peek at the website and try to follow the few requests they have listed.

# 15. THE RIVER WALK

Another tourist trap, I know, and again I'm going to tell you it is worth it to see at least once. Mostly the river is lined with shops and restaurants, but it's really pretty at night and particularly during Christmas. If you've ever seen the movie Selena, there's a bridge over the River Walk that was filmed for the movie. The River Walk is a spot of pride for San Antonio (and another item I'd be shunned for leaving out). You don't necessarily have to buy anything, either; feel free to walk the river, take in the sites, and then head out of downtown to a less touristy restaurant.

## 16. RIVER TOUR

Since you're going to visit the River Walk, you might as well do a River Tour! Personally, I'd recommend doing the boat tour around Christmas because you also get to see the Christmas Lights, so it acts as a two for one, but if you can't make it to San Antonio during the holidays, you should still do the boat tour just once.

As a current local but someone who is not from San Antonio, I can say this without any bias. The San Antonio River has some fascinating history to it. I won't spoil it for you, because that's what the river tour is for (and they'll explain it far better than I ever could), but it's worth hanging on a boat for about fifteen minutes for a quick tour of a popular tourist location and some history of the city.

# 17. MEDINA RIVER HIKING

San Antonio has quite a few hiking locations. It may be hard to see how when most of the city looks just like a city, but San Antonio has down well to preserve plenty of natural life. Medina River Natural Area has about seven miles of trails located on the 511-acre property. There are also pavilions and campsites located on the premises as well. Do be careful when hiking, especially if you're not used to the heat. Medina has excellent views and, as it is where my engagement photos were taken, has a special place in my heart. There's also a playground if you're not looking for an intense hike, but just want a day in the park.

# 18. MISSION SAN JOSÉ

Mission San José is one of the four Missions located in the San Antonio Missions National Historical Park. The Missions are about telling the stories of the people who came into the Spanish

Missions to live in the 1700s. It has a lot to do with the culture and history of San Antonio and Texas. They were not churches, but instead communities that focused on the church.

Mission San José is also known as the Queen of the Missions. It is the largest of the four and has been almost fully restored to its original design. Most notably, though, is the fact that the original Mission building defended from attack; it protected the community. Every half hour the park shoes a 23-minute film, Gente de Razon, People of Reason. The park also offers guided tours where you can learn more about the history. If you're interested, visitors may also attend mass on Sundays.

## 19. MISSION CONCEPCIÓN

The designs on the stone may have faded, but the building still stands. Mission Concepción is the oldest, unrestored stone church in America. The original founding was in 1716 and took approximately 15 years to build. It has gone through several moves to land at its final resting place in the National Historic Park. While the outside images may have faded, the inside has preserved some of the original artwork of the church.

# 20. MISSION SAN JUAN CAPISTRANO

San Juan was a self-sustaining community. Within the community, they produced tools and products. Outside of the complex they farmed and herded sheep and cattle. It wasn't long after it was built that the San Juan community became a regional supplier for produce. They had an economy that helped the mission survive attacks and epidemics. The hiking trail, guided by a park ranger, offers a unique view of the San Antonio River and the local wildlife.

# 21. MISSION ESPADA

The first Mission in Texas was Mission San Francisco de la Espada, previously San Francisco de los Tejas. Here the Native Americans learned vocational skills so that they could become Spanish citizens as the missionaries sought to make the life within the community imitate that of the Spanish villages and culture. Like many of the other Missions,

Espada did not originate where it is now located but was moved in the early 1700s.

## 22. SEAWORLD

If you're going to be in San Antonio for long enough that you would be able to make multiple visits to SeaWorld, or if you're planning on making multiple visits throughout the year, I highly recommend getting the annual pass. It typically pays for itself within two trips. There are different packages, but benefits generally include free or reduced parking, exclusive events, a percentage off in-park purchases, and the option to bring a friend on select dates. The most expensive pass also includes free reserved seating for the shows and preferred parking. The two more expensive packages also include passes to the water park, Aquatica. You don't have to go to Aquatica for a water play experience; you can cool off let your children run around in some water, SeaWorld does have the Bay of Play. It is a water playground for children that will usually have a meet-and-greet with a Sesame Street character and is located near the center of the park. Despite the perks and twelve months of access to the park, the annual passes are relatively inexpensive compared to yearly tickets for other theme parks. If you plan on doing any of the animal interactions, the park tickets have to be bought separately. If you aren't looking for more than a couple of days of visits, and you need somewhere to stay, SeaWorld has a variety of vacation packages that also include hotel stay.

The park offers a few different animal encounters, but my personal favorite is the penguin encounter. You get to spend a couple of hours in the penguin enclosure, feeding them, playing with them, and some will even let you hold or pet them. They have a professional photographer there, taking pictures so that you're free to focus on the visit and can see your photographs of the penguins after your encounter.

SeaWorld offers a few thrill rides and animal shows. Sea Lion High is my personal favorite show, though all of them are entertaining. It has puns, it has splashing, and it has otters! Recently, they've added an animal show that includes dogs, cats, birds, and pigs. If you plan your day right, you can make it to most, or all of the shows you want to see and still experience the rest of what the park has to offer.

If you plan on making an entire day of your visit, the dining pass is actually incredibly convenient and not that expensive. There's an option for just SeaWorld, or you can get the dining deal for

SeaWorld and Aquatica. The meal plan lasts for the day and includes an entrée, a side item or dessert, and a drink at least once an hour. When we go, we'll eat meals a couple of times, but we'll also use it to stay hydrated throughout the day or get a fruit cup for a snack. Just pop in, skip the meal and go for a bottle of water, and you're set. This way you do not have to lug around a bunch of food and drinks with you, you can eat and drink, and you don't have to worry about shelling out an absurd amount of money for a bottle of water.

Tip: If you're around for Christmas or Halloween, they have events for Christmas and haunted houses for Halloween.

## 23. SIX FLAGS FIESTA TEXAS

Thrill rides, carnival games, and shopping. Six Flags provides all of that and more. They, too, offer haunted houses around Halloween (but, honestly, the haunted houses at SeaWorld are better). There's generally live entertainment, most often in the form of music and shows. The lines are going to be long, so if you can avoid going in the summer (when the weather is too hot, and the kids are on summer vacation), I'd recommend that. Regardless of when you go, you'll have a blast. If you're really into thrill rides, Goliath goes at fifty miles per hour, and there's the Iron Rattler, which has dramatic drops and takes turns at seventy miles per hour. There's a long list of thrill coasters that you definitely have to try out. If you're not much into the twists and turns of roller coasters, but you do enjoy that feeling in your stomach that you get from a drop, definitely try out the Texas Gunslinger. There's a separate charge, but it's an incredible experience. You're strapped in and shot 200 feet into the air. For a brief second, you stop at that height before coming back down. The adrenaline rush is exhilarating. Six Flags also now has the first roller coaster to be named after Wonder Woman as well as being the first roller coaster that has a single rail design which provides for a smoother ride and an experience you won't get on any other roller coaster, yet.

## 24. KIDDIE PARK

The Kiddie Park is an amusement park designed for children. It has little roller coasters, a merry go round, and a few other rides. It boasts as the oldest children's amusement park in the country (though the equipment has been updated and modernized). It is an inexpensive way to spend the afternoon, and when you're finished there you're near Brackenridge Park where you can feed the ducks, or you can stop off for lunch at Cheesy Jane's. The park was first open in 1925, so it combines the elements of a fun park and some San Antonio history. The crowds usually aren't too large, and the children get an experience designed just for them--including funnel cake, mini-sized just for them. The park itself isn't very large, so you probably won't be able to make an entire day of it.

# 25. MORGAN'S WONDERLAND

Morgan's Wonderland is purportedly the world's first accessible family fun park. It is a non-profit organization that offers free admission to any guest with special needs. The theme park offers the same activities that you would find at any theme park; there is a water park (with waterproof wheelchairs available for those in batter-powered wheelchairs), there's live entertainment, you can plan parties and school trips, and rides that are designed to be accessible for adults and children. Their mission is to provide a place of play and entertainment, "regardless of age, special need or disability" and is designed for enjoyment of all individuals. The capacity of the water park is limited, it is encouraged that individuals purchase those tickets online in advance. The website does list a few hotels that are near the park and partner with Morgan's Wonderland, and using the promotional code from the park will give you a discount to the hotels on that list.

# 26. MAJESTIC THEATER

If you plan your trip in advance, you can purchase tickets to one of the many shows and musicals that are put on at the Majestic Theater, a historical landmark and the oldest theater in San Antonio. The Majestic has premiered a handful of shows and was one of the locations where the movie Selena was filmed. If you buy your tickets in advance, you can get decent seats without spending too much, and it's a great way to spend an evening in San Antonio. If you can, though, avoid parking since it is located downtown.

# 27. DOWNTOWN CARRIAGE RIDES

If you're downtown for the River Walk, or you're on a date night, or if you're just checking out what downtown has to offer, you'll find horse carriages, usually decorated with pretty lights and flowers. They're often seen wandering around the streets of downtown, and for a slight fee, you can get a tour of downtown while riding in a beautifully decorated carriage. It is generally about twenty minutes, but prices and times vary depending on the service you choose. Some businesses will offer additional services along with their rides including help with proposals, ghost tours, pick up or drop off at your hotel, or an upgrade of your carriage. I'd recommend picking your company online ahead of time, although some of the companies do offer a 'Find Your Car' option! Tell them as much as you can remember about where you parked, and they'll help you find your parking area, and give you a ride there. It will save you time and some walking.

# 28. ESCAPE ROOMS

If you've never done an escape room, but you like puzzles and mysteries, then it is something you will enjoy. Book your group ahead of time to reserve your space and one of the many San Antonio Escape Rooms will offer you an hour of trying to find your way out. Some people have the misconception that it is scary, but it isn't anything like a haunted house; nothing pops out at you, there's nothing in there meant to scare you, and you aren't wandering around to find your way out. Instead, most escape rooms have themed rooms. You'll pick your theme, and you'll be locked in for an hour. Inside that one room are the clues that lead you to keys and codes for lock combinations. Generally, you have to find the key out or answer a set of questions that will mean you've found your way out. If you come across one that is located inside a laser tag or other activity, I would pass, and instead focus on companies that are solely focused on Escape Rooms. In my experience, those were always more enjoyable.

## 29. TOWER OF AMERICAS

Nothing in San Antonio is allowed to be built taller than the Tower of Americas. You can spot the building from most freeways. At the top of the tower, there is a viewing room, which offers a view of the city, but there's also a restaurant just below the viewing room. The floor rotates, very slowly, so throughout your meal you get to experience the view of San Antonio. It is an upscale restaurant, and the food is pricey but delicious. Be sure to dress up and call ahead to book your restaurant. Chart House is the restaurant there and is one of the restaurants that participate in Restaurant Week, so if you can time your trip to coincide you can treat yourself to an expensive dinner at a lower cost. If you're not interested in the dining experience, you can purchase tickets just for the observation deck and the 4D theater ride. Dinner reservations do not include the tickets for the observation deck.

## 30. SAN ANTONIO RAMPAGE

North America has what is considered to be the strongest professional ice hockey league, with players from all over the world. The San Antonio Rampage are a minor league team, which means the tickets are cheaper, but the games are still just as much fun. We are also home to the Craziest Mascot in the American Hockey League, T-Bone. The games are held at the AT&T Center where the Spurs also play and they host dollar beer night where draft beer and sodas are only a dollar on Friday nights, which just makes the games even more enjoyable.

If you've never been to a hockey game, but you're looking for something to do, minor league is a good way to watch a live game because they're generally cheaper, and you get swept up in the excitement of the crowd. The San Antonio coach get's very into the games, and if you're sitting near enough to the glass, you can see him standing on the bench when the game is intense.

The San Antonio Rampage team make a point to have a presence in the community, fundraising for non-profit organizations, visiting schools and hospitals, and volunteering their time. They are, without a doubt, a team worth seeing.

# 31. GO SPURS GO

Visiting San Antonio, you'll see a lot of silver and black, and a lot of the slogan, "Go Spurs Go!" The Spurs play at the AT&T center and hold quite a few

NBA records as a team with the highest winning percentage in NBA history. Biggest rivals are Los Angeles Lakers, Dallas Mavericks, Houston Rockets, and Phoenix Suns, so if you happen to catch a game featuring one of those teams, hopefully, you're cheering for the Spurs!

## 32. GOLFING

Whether you're interested in amateur play or a professional golf course, San Antonio has dozens of golf courses in the city. One of the top ten courses is the Brackenridge Park Golf Course, which also happens to be the oldest public course, not just in Texas but also in San Antonio. It isn't considered a hard course, particularly for those who are experienced players, but it's one of the more entertaining courses, and it has a lot of history in Texas Golf. If you're staying near the airport, this is a great location to visit and is near the park and other activities, if not everyone in the traveling group is interested in participating in the same activities.

# 33. BRACKENRIDGE PARK

Brackenridge Park is central to several attractions in San Antonio, including the Kiddie Park, the Witte Museum, the Zoo (and the Zoo Train), the DoSeum, the Botanical Gardens, the Brackenridge Golf Course, and much more. It isn't just the location that makes it a travel spot, though. The park itself is enormous and gorgeous. It includes walking trails, playgrounds, pavilions, and multiple baseball fields. You can also feed the ducks while you're there! If you're interested in just spending the day outdoors, or taking a walk in a beautiful location, this would be the place to go.

# 34. SAN ANTONIO ZOO

I absolutely love the San Antonio Zoo. The butterfly exhibit is pretty cool, although it does have an additional (but cheap) charge from your entrance. My favorite thing about the zoo, though, is Lorie Landing. This is for all bird lovers. Lorie Landing is the bird enclosure that you can go into and hang out with the birds. They are so friendly and used to people, that they will often come right up to you. If you pay a small fee, you can buy the syrup that they like, in these little cups and you can entice them onto your arm (or in my case my head), and they'll eat their treat while perched on you. It's a fun experience that I've never had at any other zoo I've been to. There is also the Zoo Train that goes around the zoo and through Brackenridge Park. You can feed the giraffes three times a day, or pay extra for a behind the scenes interaction with the tortoise, rhino, or hippo. I think going to the zoo is an underrated activity. You get to learn about the different animals, see some cool animals, and just spend an afternoon outdoors, and it isn't too costly.

## 35. JAPANESE TEA GARDENS

A public park, the Japanese Tea Gardens came from land donated in 1899 and is built on an old quarry. The gardens have a fascinating history as the quarry was shaped through prison labor. In 1926 the Bamboo Room opened up serving light lunches and tea, and the little restaurant still exists there today. During World War II, there was a strong anti-Japanese sentiment in America, and the tea gardens were renamed to the Chinese Sunken Garden. However, in 1984 a ceremony was held, and the name once more reverted back to the Japanese Tea Gardens. Now, you can visit the beautiful scenery (for free!), take in the Japanese landscape, and learn a little about the history.

## 36. MCNAY ART MUSEUM

A museum in a mansion, the McNay Art Museum hosts American and European art that range from Medieval to contemporary works. The estate itself is historic, built in 1929. Aside from the art on display, the museum acts as a wedding or event venue, offers curatorial internships, allows for photography sessions, and offers a variety of guided tours around the museum.

## 37. THE WITTE MUSEUM

Every Tuesday, general admission to the museum is free. On top of the exhibits, the Witte offers special events, like Culinary Nights, throughout the month that will sometimes include access into one of the special exhibits. The displays are generally designed really well, and the addition of events throughout the month can make the Witte an uncommon experience.

## 38. EISENHOWER PARK

Another excellent location for hiking, and spending the day outdoors; Eisenhower Park has hiking trails just a little over six miles, pavilion locations, and playgrounds. If a long hike doesn't appeal to you, there are smaller trails that are meant more for family walking or jogging rather than hiking; regardless of your hiking experience or interest, there are a couple of different trails that you can choose from. Most of the path is natural, although some parts have been paved. At the peak of the trail, there is an observation tower that hikers can use that looks over the tops of the trees and overs a view of the park.

## 39. WILDLIFE RANCH

The next three items on the list are not technically in San Antonio. Wildlife Ranch and Natural Bridge Caverns are in New Braunfels, and Enchanted Rock is just past Fredericksburg. However, they are just a short—and scenic!—drive from San Antonio, and so they make a fun day trip from the city.

Wildlife Ranch isn't too expensive, but I wouldn't recommend taking a rental car. You pay to enter, and you buy food for the animals. Then, you drive along the route, and you can stop along the path at any point if you're fond of a particular animal. Most of them will come right up to your car, and you can throw them food or, if you're feeling brave enough and depending on the animal), offer them food straight from your bag. They don't recommend you feeding the zebras directly, because they have such big teeth. We fed them from the bag, and the zebra ended up taking the entire bag, spilling most of the food, and eating the paper.

The whole encounter is neat, and they have a restaurant, gift shop, and bathrooms near the end of the trail, so you don't even have to leave to find something to eat.

# 40. NATURAL BRIDGE CAVERNS

Wear shoes and clothes you are comfortable walking in. You can check the website to see what the temperature is going to be like inside the cavern so that you might dress appropriately. Keep in mind; most of the tours do require a lot of walking. However, Natural Bridge Caverns doesn't just offer tours of the caverns; there are plenty of other things to do while you're there, and activities that are well-suited for all ages.

## 41. ENCHANTED ROCK

Enchanted Rock is a state park that is located north of Fredericksburg, Texas. It's a day trip from San Antonio, but the park holds the second largest granite batholith in the United States. If you're interested in hiking, this is a long, very steep eleven miles to climb, but the view of the Hill Country from up top is incredible. There's also a small cave you can climb around in, once you make it to the top. If you're not interested in making the journey, the park does offer camping, rock climbing, and shopping as well. On your way in, or if you're not too tired, you can stop on your way out, visit Fredericksburg. It's a tiny, German town with museums, shopping, and dining options.

# 42. RIPLEY'S BELIEVE IT OR NOT ODDITORIUM AND WAX MUSEUM

Who doesn't love a museum where you can actually touch stuff? If you like learning about world records and collections of bizarre things, then this is the museum for you. Longest nails in history, wax figures of famous people, shrunken heads, and there's a 4D theater where your seat moves with the movie. It's a strange world we live in, and this place is even stranger. You can purchase single tickets to each attraction, or if you're interested in more of the Ripley experience, you can buy tickets as a combo ticket that can include two or more of the attractions.

# 43. RIPLEY'S HAUNTED ADVENTURE AND TOMB RIDER

With the Odditorium, Ripley's has the haunted house and the fun ride, Tomb Rider. I've never actually done the haunted house because the one time we went, my party didn't want to go, but it does look like a lot of fun, and because it is at Ripley's, it's bound to be strange and probably scary. Tomb Rider is a 3D, special effect ride with laser guns you get to shoot while you ride. After the ride is an arcade of games, and if you're interested in riding again, the re-rides are very cheap.

## 44. SAN ANTONIO FIRE MUSEUM

Located near the Alamo, the museum displays trucks and equipment used by the fire department throughout history. They are always getting new stuff and changing their display, so every visit is bound to be different. They also have a kid's area, a 1953 fire truck that children can climb on and wear a replica of firefighter gear, an EMS display, and a theater that shows videos of the history of firefighters and information about their training today. They have equipment dating back to the 1800s! It is not a very long outing, so don't plan to spend the entire day here, but it is something unique to San Antonio.

# 45. UNIVERSITY OF INCARNATE WORD LIGHT THE WAY

Around Christmas, the University of Incarnate Words decorates the school, and it is available for people to drive through and look at the Christmas lights. It used to be just decorations, but as the event has grown, it has become more of a festival. The event is sponsored by the local grocery store, H.E.B, and the lights come on following a ceremony hosted by a local news station. Also present are food trucks and performance with the kick off night ending with fireworks. The school also collects unused toys around this time to donate. Admission is free and has more to do than most neighborhoods you might drive through to check out the lights.

# 46. SAN ANTONIO AQUARIUM

As far as aquariums go, this one is slightly underwhelming. It does have a feeding area, an aviary, and inflatable play area, but aside from that, there's not much about it to make it a desirable visit. Unlike everything on this list, this is more of a recommendation of somewhere not to visit. It might kill a couple of hours, looking at the fish but you're better off going to the aquarium at SeaWorld. They do, however, allow foster children and children under two in for free.

# 47. BRISCOE WESTERN ART MUSEUM

This is focused on the art and history of the American West; cowboys, John Wayne, and creativity of the time period. They also host events, during the summer they offer a western film series and have a day for preschool-aged children to listen to stories and make art. Admission is relatively inexpensive with a discount available for students. The museum is dedicated to sharing the culture of the west and will also engage in public events meant to share and educate on the history.

# 48. BOTANICAL GARDENS

Admission is cheap, with the option for a student discount, and you can spend as long as you like. You're welcome to bring a picnic, and some days are designated for being able to bring your dogs. Also located within the gardens is an opportunity for bird watching, and a gift shop. Whether you're really into plant-life, or you don't know the names of the flowers but you just like looking at them, this is an enjoyable way to spend an afternoon, or you can rent the garden for your own event including weddings, receptions, birthdays, etc. If you do plan on hosting an event at the gardens, Ann Maries is on their list of caterers, and they do a fantastic job with reasonable pricing.

# 49. DOSEUM

Admission is cheap, with the option for a student discount, and you can spend as long as you like. You're welcome to bring a picnic, and some days are designated for being able to bring your dogs. Also located within the gardens is an opportunity for bird watching, and a gift shop. Whether you're really into plant-life, or you don't know the names of the flowers but you just like looking at them, this is an enjoyable way to spend an afternoon, or you can rent the garden for your own event including weddings, receptions, birthdays, etc. If you do plan on hosting an event at the gardens, Ann Maries is on their list of caterers, and they do a fantastic job with reasonable pricing.

# 50. SHOPPING

Lone Star Mall, La Cantera, The Rim, and the Pearl Brewery Farmer's Market are enjoyable locations for shopping. The Farmer's Market has over forty vendors every weekend. They sell the usual produce and homemade salsas and things you might also find at a farmer's market, anywhere, but you can also buy food you can enjoy while walking around. One weekend I went, there was a stand selling chicken and waffles. The bakeries and restaurants in the area are also usually open early for the farmer's market, so if you're looking for a break from exploring the vendors, there are some unique places nearby to try out.

Lone Star Mall, La Cantera, and The Rim have the usual stores you find at malls. They also happen to be located near some pretty cool places. La Cantera and The Rim are near one another, on opposite sides of the freeway. They're located near Six Flags and near a handful of restaurants. If you're looking to eat somewhere more familiar, Olive Garden, Red Lobster, and other chain restaurants are nearby.

# TOP REASONS TO BOOK THIS TRIP

**Food**: Texas food has a flavor and approach that is often different than most other states. Within Texas you can find a variety of takes on the same dish.

**Shopping**: Nearly every activity in this book includes shopping in it. So, even if you're not interested in hiking or theme parks, you can compromise with your traveling companions and get some shopping in. There's honestly something for everyone.

**History**: Most of the items on this list are filled with historical places. Nearly everything in San Antonio goes back with some kind of historical significance or story. I think it is pretty cool to experience some of the things that existed in the city early on.

# BONUS BOOK

# 50 THINGS TO KNOW ABOUT PACKING LIGHT FOR TRAVEL

## PACK THE RIGHT WAY EVERY TIME

AUTHOR: MANIDIPA BHATTACHARYYA

Edited by Melanie Howthorne

## ABOUT THE AUTHOR

Manidipa Bhattacharyya is a creative writer and editor, with an education in English literature and Linguistics. After working in the IT industry for seven long years she decided to call it quits and follow her heart instead. Manidipa has been ghost writing, editing, proof reading and doing secondary research services for many story tellers and article writers for about three years. She stays in Kolkata, India with her husband and a busy two year old. In her own time Manidipa enjoys travelling, photography and writing flash fiction.

Manidipa believes in travelling light and never carries anything that she couldn't haul herself on a trip. However, travelling with her child changed the scenario. She seemed to carry the entire world with her for the baby on the first two trips. But good sense prevailed and she is again working her way to becoming a light traveler, this time with a kid.

# INTRODUCTION

*He who would travel happily*
*must travel light.*

-Antoine de Saint-Exupéry

Travel takes you to different places from seas and mountains to deserts and much more. In your travels you get to interact with different people and their cultures. You will, however, enjoy the sights and interact positively with these new people even more, if you are travelling light.

When you travel light your mind can be free from worry about your belongings. You do not have to spend precious vacation time waiting for your luggage to arrive after a long flight. There is be no chance of your bags going missing and the best part is that you need not pay a fee for checked baggage.

People who have mastered this art of packing light will root for you to take only one carry-on, wherever you go. However, many people can find it really hard to pack light. More so if you are travelling with children. Differentiating between "must have" and "just in case" items is the starting point. There will be ample shopping avenues at your destination which are just waiting to be explored.

This book will show you 'packing' in a new 'light' – pun intended – and help you to embrace light packing practices for all of your future travels.

Off to packing!

# DEDICATION

I dedicate this book to all the travel buffs that I know, who have given me great insights into the contents of their backpacks.

# THE RIGHT TRAVEL GEAR

## 1. CHOOSE YOUR TRAVEL GEAR CAREFULLY

While selecting your travel gear, pick items that are light weight, durable and most importantly, easy to carry. There are cases with wheels so you can drag them along – these are usually on the heavy side because of the trolley. Alternatively a backpack that you can carry comfortably on your back, or even a duffel bag that you can carry easily by hand or sling across your body are also great options. Whatever you choose, one thing to keep in mind is that the luggage itself should not weigh a ton, this will give you the flexibility to bring along one extra pair of shoes if you so desire.

## 2. CARRY THE MINIMUM NUMBER OF BAGS

Selecting light weight luggage is not everything. You need to restrict the number of bags you carry as well. One carry-on size bag is ideal for light travel. Most carriers allow one cabin baggage plus one purse, handbag or camera bag as long as it slides under the seat in front. So technically, you can carry two items of luggage without checking them in.

## 3. PACK ONE EXTRA BAG

Always pack one extra empty bag along with your essential items. This could be a very light weight duffel bag or even a sturdy tote bag which takes up minimal space. In the event that you end up buying a lot of souvenirs, you already have a handy bag to stuff all that into and do not have to spend time hunting for an appropriate bag.

*I'm very strict with my packing and have everything in its right place. I never change a rule. I hardly use anything in the hotel room. I wheel my own wardrobe in and that's it.*

Charlie Watts

# CLOTHES & ACCESSORIES

## 4. PLAN AHEAD

Figure out in advance what you plan to do on your trip. That will help you to pick that one dress you need for the occasion. If you are going to attend a wedding then you have to carry formal wear. If not, you can ditch the gown for something lighter that will be comfortable during long walks or on the beach.

## 5. WEAR THAT JACKET

Remember that wearing items will not add extra luggage for your air travel. So wear that bulky jacket that you plan to carry for your trip. This saves space and can also help keep you warm during the chilly flight.

## 6. MIX AND MATCH

Carry clothes that can be interchangeably used to reinvent your look. Find one top that goes well with a couple of pairs of pants or skirts. Use tops, shirts and jackets wisely along with other accessories like a scarf or a stole to create a new look.

## 7. CHOOSE YOUR FABRIC WISELY

Stuffing clothes in cramped bags definitely takes its toll which results in wrinkles. It is best to carry wrinkle free, synthetic clothes or merino tops. This will eliminate the need for that small iron you usually bring along.

## 8. DITCH CLOTHES PACK UNDERWEAR

Pack more underwear and socks. These are the things that will give you a fresh feel even if you do not get a chance to wear fresh clothes. Moreover these are easy to wash and can be dried inside the hotel room itself.

## 9. CHOOSE DARK OVER LIGHT

While picking your clothes choose dark coloured ones. They are easy to colour coordinate and can last longer before needing a wash. Accidental food spills and dirt from the road are less visible on darker clothes.

## 10. WEAR YOUR JEANS

Take only one pair of Jeans with you, which you should wear on the flight. Remember to pick a pair that can be worn for sightseeing trips and is equally eloquent for dinner. You can add variety by adding light weight cargoes and chinos.

## 11. CARRY SMART ACCESSORIES

The right accessory can give you a fresh look even with the same old dress. An intelligent neck-piece, a couple of bright scarves, stoles or a sarong can be used in a number of ways to add variety to your clothing. These light weight beauties can double up as a nursing cover, a light blanket, beach wear, a modesty cover for visiting places of worship, and also makes for an enthralling game of peek-a-boo.

## 12. LEARN TO FOLD YOUR GARMENTS

Seasoned travellers all swear by rolling their clothes for compact and wrinkle free packing. Bundle packing, where you roll the clothes around a central object as if tying it up, is also a popular method of compact and wrinkle free packing. Stacking folded clothes one on top of another is a big no-no as it makes creases extreme and they are difficult to get rid of without ironing.

## 13. WASH YOUR DIRTY LAUNDRY

One of the ways to avoid carrying loads of clothes is to wash the clothes you carry. At some places you might get to use the laundry services or a Laundromat but if you are in a pinch, best solution is to wash them yourself. If that is the plan then carrying quick drying clothes is highly recommended, which most often also happen to be the wrinkle free variety.

## 14. LEAVE THOSE TOWELS BEHIND

Regular towels take up a lot of space, are heavy and take ages to dry out. If you are staying at hotels they will provide you with towels anyway. If you are travelling to a remote place, where the availability of towels look doubtful, carry a light weight travel towel of viscose material to do the job.

## 15. USE A COMPRESSION BAG

Compression bags are getting lots of recommendation now days from regular travellers. These are useful for saving space in your luggage when you have to pack bulky dresses. While packing for the return trip, get help from the hotel staff to arrange a vacuum cleaner.

# FOOTWEAR

## 16. PUT ON YOUR HIKING BOOTS

If you have plans to go hiking or trekking during your trip, you will need those bulky hiking boots. The best way to carry them is to wear them on flight to save space and luggage weight. You can remove the boots once inside and be comfortable in your socks.

## 17. PICKING THE RIGHT SHOES

Shoes are often the bulkiest items, along with being the dainty if you are a female. They need care and take up a lot of space in your luggage. It is advisable therefore to pick shoes very carefully. If you plan to do a lot of walking and site seeing, then wearing a pair of comfortable walking shoes are a must. For more formal occasions you can carry durable, light weight flats which will not take up much space.

## 18. STUFF SHOES

If you happen to pack a pair of shoes, ensure you utilize their hollow insides. Tuck small items like rolled up socks or belts to save space. They will also be easy to find.

# TOILETRIES

## 19. STASHING TOILETRIES

Carry only absolute necessities. Airline rules dictate that for one carry-on bag, liquids and gels must be in 3.4 ounce (100ml) bottles or less, and must be packed in a one quart zip-lock bag. If you are planning to stay in a hotel, the basic things will be provided for you. It's best is to buy the rest from the local market at your destination.

## 20. TAKE ALONG TAMPONS

Tampons are a hard to find item in a lot of countries. Figure out how many you need and pack accordingly. For longer stays you can buy them online and have them delivered to where you are staying.

## 21. GET PAMPERED BEFORE YOU TRAVEL

Some avid travellers suggest getting a pedicure and manicure just the day before travelling. This not only gives you a well kept look, you also save the trouble of packing nail polish. Remember, every little bit of weight reduced adds up.

# ELECTRONICS

## 22. LUGGING ALONG ELECTRONICS

Electronics have a large role to play in our lives today. Most of us cannot imagine our lives away from our phones, laptops or tablets. However while travelling, one must consider the amount of weight these electronics add to our luggage. Thankfully smart phones come along with all the essentials tools like a camera, email access, picture editing tools and more. They are smart to the point of eliminating the need to carry multiple gadgets. Choose a smart phone that suits all your requirements and travel with the world in your palms or pocket.

## 23. REDUCE THE NUMBER OF CHARGERS

If you do travel with multiple electronic devices, you will have to bear the additional burden of carrying all their chargers too. Check if a single charger can be used for multiple devices. You might also consider investing in a pocket charger. These small devices support multiple devices while keeping you charged on the go.

# 24. TRAVEL FRIENDLY APPS

Along with smart phones come numerous apps, which are immensely helpful in our travels. You name it and you have an app for it at hand – take pictures, sharing with friends and family, torch to light dark roads, maps, checking flight/train times, find hotels and many other things. Use these smart alternatives to traditional items like books to eliminate weight and save space.

*I get ideas about what's essential when packing my suitcase.*

-Diane von Furstenberg

# TRAVELLING WITH KIDS

# 25. BRING ALONG THE STROLLER

Kids might enjoy walking for a while but they soon tire out and a stroller is the just the right thing for them to rest in while you continue your tour. Strollers also double duty as a luggage carrier and shopping bag holder. Remember to pick a light weight, easy to handle brand of stroller. Better yet, find out in advance if you can rent a stroller at your destination.

## 26. BRING ONLY ENOUGH DIAPERS FOR YOUR TRIP

Diapers take up a lot of space and add to the weight of your luggage. Therefore it is advisable to carry just enough diapers to last through the trip and a few for afterwards, till you buy fresh stock at your destination. Unless of course you are travelling to a really remote area, in which case you have no choice but to carry the load. Otherwise diapers are something you will find pretty easily.

## 27. TAKE ONLY A COUPLE OF TOYS

Children are easily attracted by new things in their environment. While travelling they will find numerous 'new' objects to scrutinize and play with. Packing just one favorite toy is enough, or if there is no favorite toy leave out all of them in favor of stories or imaginary games.

## 28. CARRY KID FRIENDLY SNACKS

Create a small snack counter in your bag to store away quick bites for those sudden hunger pangs. Depending on the child's age this could include chocolates, raisins, dry fruits, granola bars or biscuits. Also keep a bottle of water handy for your little one. These things do not add much weight and can be adjusted in a handbag or knapsack.

# 29. GAMES TO CARRY

Create some travel specific, imaginary games if you have slightly grown up children, like spot the attractions. Keep a coloring book and colors handy for in-flight or hotel time. Apps on your smart phone can keep the children engaged with cartoons and story books. Older children are often entertained by games available on phones or tablets. This cuts the weight of luggage down while keeping the kids entertained.

# 30. LET THE KIDS CARRY THEIR LOAD

A good thing is to start early sharing of responsibilities. Let your child pick a bag of his or her choice and pack it themselves. Keep tabs on what they are stuffing in their bags by asking if they will be using that item on the trip. It could start out being just an entertainment bag initially but with growing years they will learn to sort the useful from the superfluous. Children as little as four can maneuver a small trolley suitcase like a pro- their experience in pull along toys credit. If you are worried that you may be pulling it for them, you may want to start with a backpack.

## 31. DECIDE ON LOCATION FOR CHILDREN TO SLEEP

While on a trip you might not always get a crib at your destination, and carrying one will make life all the more difficult. Instead call ahead to see if there are any cribs or roll out beds for children. You may even put blankets on the floor. Weave them a story about camping and they will gladly sleep without any trouble.

## 32. GET BABY PRODUCTS DELIVERED AT YOUR DESTINATION

If you are absolutely paranoid about not getting your favourite variety of diaper or brand of baby food, check out online stores like amazon.com for services in your destination city. You can buy things online ahead of your travel and get them delivered to your hotel upon arrival.

## 33. FEEDING NEEDS OF YOUR INFANTS

If you are travelling with a breastfed infant, you save the trouble of carrying bottles and bottle sanitization kits. For special food, or medications, you may need to call ahead to make sure you have a refrigerator where you are staying.

# 34. FEEDING NEEDS OF YOUR TODDLER

With the progression from infancy to toddler, their dietary requirements too evolve. You will have to pack some snacks for travelling time. Fresh fruits and vegetables can be purchased at your destination. Most of the cities you travel to in whichever part of the world, will have baby food products and formulas, available at the local drug-store or the supermarket.

# 35. PICKING CLOTHES FOR YOUR BABY

Contrary to popular belief, babies can do without many changes of clothes. At the most pack 2 outfits per day. Pack mix and match type clothes for your little one as well. Pick things which are comfortable to wear and quick to dry.

# 36. SELECTING SHOES FOR YOUR BABY

Like outfits, kids can make do with two pairs of comfortable shoes. If you can get some water resistant shoes it will be best. To expedite drying wet shoes, you can stuff newspaper in them then wrap them with newspaper and leave them to dry overnight.

## 37. KEEP ONE CHANGE OF CLOTHES HANDY

Travelling with kids can be tricky. Keep a change of clothes for the kids and mum handy in your purse or tote bag. This takes a bit of space in your hand luggage but comes extremely handy in case there are any accidents or spills.

## 38. LEAVE BEHIND BABY ACCESSORIES

Baby accessories like their bed, bath tub, car seat, crib etc. should be left at home. Many hotels provide a crib on request, while car seats can be borrowed from friends or rented. Babies can be given a bath in the hotel sink or even in the adult bath tub with a little bit of water. If you bring a few bath toys, they can be used in the bath, pool, and out of water. They can also be sanitized easily in the sink.

## 39. CARRY A SMALL LOAD OF PLASTIC BAGS

With children around there are chances of a number of soiled clothes and diapers. These plastic bags help to sort the dirt from the clean inside your big bag. These are very light weight and come in handy to other carry stuff as well at times.

# PACK WITH A PURPOSE

## 40. PACKING FOR BUSINESS TRIPS

One neutral-colored suit should suffice. It can be paired with different shirts, ties and accessories for different occasions. One pair of black suit pants could be worn with a matching jacket for the office or with a snazzy top for dinner.

## 41. PACKING FOR A CRUISE

Most cruises have formal dinners, and that formal dress usually takes up a lot of space. However you might find a tuxedo to rent. For women, a short black dress with multiple accessory options will do the trick.

## 42. PACKING FOR A LONG TRIP OVER DIFFERENT CLIMATES

The secret packing mantra for travel over multiple climates is layering. Layering traps air around your body creating insulation against the cold. The same light t-shirt that is comfortable in a warmer climate can be the innermost layer in a colder climate.

# REDUCE SOME MORE WEIGHT

## 43. LEAVE PRECIOUS THINGS AT HOME

Things that you would hate to lose or get damaged leave them at home. Precious jewelry, expensive gadgets or dresses, could be anything. You will not require these on your trip. Leave them at home and spare the load on your mind.

## 44. SEND SOUVENIRS BY MAIL

If you have spent all your money on purchasing souvenirs, carrying them back in the same bag that you brought along would be difficult. Either pack everything in another bag and check it in the airport or get everything shipped to your home. Use an international carrier for a secure transit, but this could be more expensive than the checking fees at the airport.

## 45. AVOID CARRYING BOOKS

Books equal to weight. There are many reading apps which you can download on your smart phone or tab. Plus there are gadgets like Kindle and Nook that are thinner and lighter alternatives to your regular book.

# CHECK, GET, SET, CHECK AGAIN

## 46. STRATEGIZE BEFORE PACKING

Create a travel list and prepare all that you think you need to carry along. Keep everything on your bed or floor before packing and then think through once again – do I really need that? Any item that meets this question can be avoided. Remove whatever you don't really need and pack the rest.

## 47. TEST YOUR LUGGAGE

Once you have fully packed for the trip take a test trip with your luggage. Take your bags and go to town for window shopping for an hour. If you enjoy your hour long trip it is good to go, if not, go home and reduce the load some more. Repeat this test till you hit the right weight.

## 48. ADD A ROLL OF DUCT TAPE

You might wonder why, when this book has been talking about reducing stuff, we're suddenly asking you to pack something totally unusual. This is because when you have limited supplies, duct tape is immensely helpful for small repairs – a broken bag, leaking zip-lock bag, broken sunglasses, you name it and duct tape can fix it, temporarily.

# 49. LIST OF ESSENTIAL ITEMS

Even though the emphasis is on packing light, there are things which have to be carried for any trip. Here is our list of essentials:

- Passport/Visa or any other ID
- Any other paper work that might be required on a trip like permits, hotel reservation confirmations etc.
- Medicines – all your prescription medicines and emergency kit, especially if you are travelling with children
- Medical or vaccination records
- Money in foreign currency if travelling to a different country
- Tickets- Email or Message them to your phone

# 50. MAKE THE MOST OF YOUR TRIP

Wherever you are going, whatever you hope to do we encourage you to embrace it whole-heartedly. Take in the scenery, the culture and above all, enjoy your time away from home.

# PACKING AND PLANNING TIPS

**A Week before Leaving**

- Arrange for someone to take care of pets and water plants
- Stop mail and newspaper
- Notify Credit Card companies where you are going.
- Change your thermostat settings
- Car inspected, oil is changed, and tires have the correct pressure.
- Passports and id is up to date.
- Pay bills.
- Copy important items and download travel Apps.
- Start collecting small bills for tips
- Clean out refrigerator.
- Empty garbage cans.
- Lock windows.
- Make sure you have the right ID with you.
- Bring cash for tips.
- Remember travel documents.
- Lock door behind you.
- Remember wallet.
- Unplug items in house and pack chargers.

# READ OTHER GREATER THAN A TOURIST BOOKS

Greater Than a Tourist San Miguel de Allende Guanajuato Mexico: 50 Travel Tips from a Local by Tom Peterson

Greater Than a Tourist – Lake George Area New York USA: 50 Travel Tips from a Local by Janine Hirschklau

Greater Than a Tourist – Monterey California United States: 50 Travel Tips from a Local by Katie Begley

Greater Than a Tourist – Chanai Crete Greece: 50 Travel Tips from a Local by Dimitra Papagrigoraki

Greater Than a Tourist – The Garden Route Western Cape Province South Africa: 50 Travel Tips from a Local by Li-Anne McGregor van Aardt

Greater Than a Tourist – Sevilla Andalusia Spain: 50 Travel Tips from a Local by Gabi Gazon

Greater Than a Tourist – Kota Bharu Kelantan Malaysia: 50 Travel Tips from a Local by Aditi Shukla

Children's Book: Charlie the Cavalier Travels the World by Lisa Rusczyk

# > TOURIST

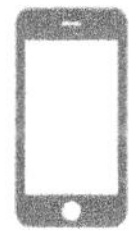

Visit Greater Than a Tourist for Free Travel Tips http://GreaterThanATourist.com

Sign up for the Greater Than a Tourist Newsletter for discount days, new books, and travel information: http://eepurl.com/cxspyf

Follow us on Facebook for tips, images, and ideas: https://www.facebook.com/GreaterThanATourist

Follow us on Pinterest for travel tips and ideas: http://pinterest.com/GreaterThanATourist

Follow us on Instagram for beautiful travel images: http://Instagram.com/GreaterThanATourist

# > TOURIST

Please leave your honest review of this book on Amazon and Goodreads. Please send your feedback to GreaterThanaTourist@gmail.com as we continue to improve the series. Thank you. We appreciate your positive and constructive feedback. Thank you.

# METRIC CONVERSIONS

## TEMPERATURE

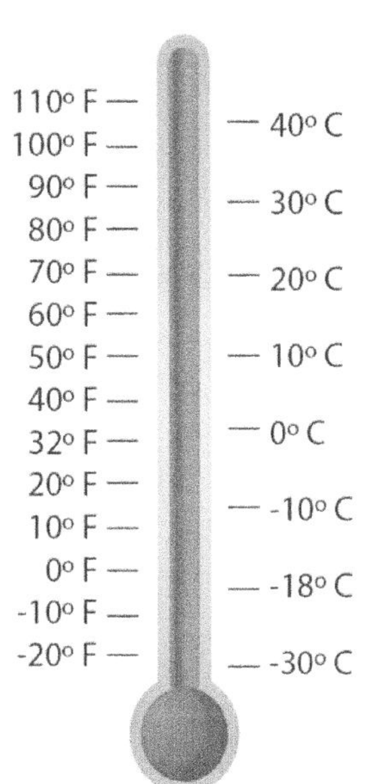


*To convert F to C:*

*Subtract 32, and then multiply by 5/9 or .5555.*

*To Convert C to F:*

*Multiply by 1.8 and then add 32.*

*32F = 0C*

## LIQUID VOLUME

***To Convert:...................Multiply by***

*U.S. Gallons to Liters................ 3.8*

*U.S. Liters to Gallons ................26*

*Imperial Gallons to U.S. Gallons 1.2*

*Imperial Gallons to Liters....... 4.55*

*Liters to Imperial Gallons ........22*

***1 Liter = .26 U.S. Gallon***

***1 U.S. Gallon = 3.8 Liters***

## DISTANCE

***To convert ............Multiply by***

*Inches to Centimeters ....2.54*

*Centimeters to Inches ........39*

*Feet to Meters...................... .3*

*Meters to Feet ..................3.28*

*Yards to Meters ..................91*

*Meters to Yards ................1.09*

*Miles to Kilometers ..........1.61*

*Kilometers to Miles............ .62*

***1 Mile = 1.6 km***

***1 km = .62 Miles***

## WEIGHT

*1 Ounce = .28 Grams*

*1 Pound = .4555 Kilograms*

*1 Gram = .04 Ounce*

*1 Kilogram = 2.2 Pounds*

# TRAVEL QUESTIONS

- Do you bring presents home to family or friends after a vacation?
- Do you get motion sick?
- Do you have a favorite billboard?
- Do you know what to do if there is a flat tire?
- Do you like a sun roof open?
- Do you like to eat in the car?
- Do you like to wear sun glasses in the car?
- Do you like toppings on your ice cream?
- Do you use public bathrooms?
- Did you bring your cell phone and does it have power?
- Do you have a form of identification with you?
- Have you ever been pulled over by a cop?
- Have you ever given money to a stranger on a road trip?
- Have you ever taken a road trip with animals?
- Have you ever went on a vacation alone?
- Have you ever run out of gas?

- If you could move to any place in the world, where would it be?
- If you could travel anywhere in the world, where would you travel?
- If you could travel in any vehicle, which one would it be?
- If you had three things to wish for from a magic genie, what would they be?
- If you have a driver's license, how many times did it take you to pass the test?
- What are you the most afraid of on vacation?
- What do you want to get away from the most when you are on vacation?
- What foods smells bad to you?
- What item to you bring on ever trip with you away from home?
- What makes you sleepy?
- What song would you love to hear on the radio when you're cruising on the highway?
- What travel job would you want the least?
- What will you miss most while you are away from home?
- What is something you always wanted to try?

- What is the best road side attraction that you ever saw?
- What is the farthest distance you ever biked?
- What is the farthest distance you ever walked?
- What is the weirdest thing you needed to buy while on vacation?
- What is your favorite candy?
- What is your favorite color car?
- What is your favorite family vacation?
- What is your favorite food in the world?
- What is your favorite gas station drink or food?
- What is your favorite license plate design?
- What is your favorite restaurant in the world?
- What is your favorite smell?
- What is your favorite song?
- What is your favorite sound that nature makes?
- What is your favorite thing to bring home from a vacation?
- What is your favorite vacation with friends?
- What is your favorite way to relax?

- What is your favorite weather conditions while driving?
- Where in the world would you rather never get to travel?
- Where is the farthest place you ever traveled in a car?
- Where is the farthest place you ever went North, South, East and West?
- Where is your favorite place in the world?
- Who is your favorite singer?
- Who taught you how to drive?
- Who will you miss the most while you are away?
- Who if the first person you will call when you get to your destination?
- Who brought you on your first vacation?
- Who likes to travel the most in your life?
- Would you rather be hot or cold?
- Would you rather drive above, below, or at the speed limited?
- Would you rather drive on a highway or a back road?
- Would you rather go on a train or a boat?
- Would you rather go to the beach or the woods?

# TRAVEL BUCKET LIST

# NOTES

Made in the USA
Monee, IL
23 May 2022

96940473R00062